100 WORDS Kids Need to Read by 3rd Grade

Sight word practice to build strong readers

from the editors of Scholastic News

Scholastic
Professional Books

New York • Toronto • London • Auckland • Sydney

Contents

Dear Educator,

Teachers know and experts agree that the only way for children to master sight words—those high frequency, often non-decodable words essential to reading fluency—is through practice. With *100 Words Kids Need to Read,* we are pleased to offer a tool to help provide that practice in an engaging, effective format.

We created the three books in this series—for first, second, and third graders—with the guidance of literacy experts and classroom teachers. Broken down into manageable groups, words are introduced in context and reinforced through inviting puzzles and games. Each sequence of activities is carefully designed to touch on reading, writing, and usage, taking children beyond mere visual recognition of sight words to genuine mastery.

The journey through these skill-building pages will help young readers make the successful transition from learning to read to reading to learn. Along the way, they will also receive excellent preparation for standardized tests. Enjoy the trip!

David Goddy
VP, Publisher

ANSWER KEY **p. 4:** 2. write; 3. tell; 4. wrote; 5. believe; 6. could, should **p. 5:** would; these; those; believes; could; enough; know; answer; *the sidewalk* **p. 6:** 2. know; 3. answers; 4. would; 5. believe; 6. writing; 7. tell; 8. enough **p. 7:** 2. walk; 3. bought; 4. bring; 5. draw; 6. hold; 7. talk; 8. drew **p. 8:** 2. held; 3. talk; 4. think; 5. buy; 6. laugh; 7. hurt **p. 9:** 1. Lilly drew a picture. 2. Sam held his nose. 3. Jake thought hard. 4. Sam wrote a letter. 5. Jake laughed at Sam's joke. 6. Jake bought some candy. 7. Lilly brought Pete to school. 8. Lilly and Pete walked home. 9. My head hurts. **p. 10:** 5. because; 6. through; 7. around; 1. far; 2. below; 4. very; 5. behind **p. 11:** 1. A bird flew with a worm in her mouth. 2. I saw her fly into her nest. 3. She fed her babies so they would grow. 4. When they were done, she got more food. 5. A mother bird does a lot of work! 6. I began going to see them every day. 7. The babies grew and flew away. **p. 12:** because; going; through; around; grew; above; behind; done; flew; does **p. 13:** 2. start; 3. always; 4. its; 5. may; 6. year; 7. right **p. 14:** month; always; never; must; light; just; *Cheer him up* **p. 15:** 1. b; 2. r. 3. e; 4. a; 5. t; 6. h; *Your breath* **p. 16:** 2. call; 3. full; 4. away; 5. upon; 6. pull **p. 17:** 1. b; 2. a; 3. c; 4. c; 5. a **p. 18:** *Action:* call, find, put, pull; *Direction:* away, below, upon, around, behind, above **p. 19:** 1. word; 3. clean; 4. warm; 5. ready; 2. own; 3. carry; 6. again **p. 20:** Answers will vary. **p. 21:** 2. clean; 3. owns; 4. ready; 5. carried; 6. about; 7. middle; 8. sure **p. 22:** Neither; been; several; yesterday; Today; either; different; tomorrow. *Now try this!* different, either, neither, several, today; together, tomorrow, yesterday **p. 23:** 1. Another word for trouble is difficulty. 2. The opposite of beautiful is ugly. 3. Another word for beautiful is pretty. 4. Frighten means the same as scare. 5. To learn, one must study or practice. 6. Straight rhymes with eight. 7. In this story, straight means directly. **p. 24:** 1. trouble; 2. been; 3. together; 4. learn; 5. several; 6. different; 7. beautiful; 8. tomorrow; 9. today

Editor: Kaaren Sorensen **Art Directors:** Deborah Dinger, Joan Michael, Beth Benzaquin **Editorial Consultants:** Wiley Blevins, Mary C. Rose, Sue Sxczepanski **Writers:** Spencer Kayden, Jessica B. Levine **Copy Editors:** L.C. Israel, Bryan Brown •**Magazine Group**: VP, Publisher: David Goddy•VP, Editor in Chief: Rebecca Bondor•Associate Editorial Director: Alyse Sweeney•Design Director: Judith Christ-Lafond• Production Director: Barbara Schwartz•Executive Director of Photography: Steven Diamond•Publishing System Director: David Hendrickson•Manager, Digital Imaging Group: Marc Stern•Director of Library Service: Bert Schacter•Library Manager: Maggie Stevaralgia•VP, Marketing: Jocelyn Forman•**Scholastic Education**: President: Margery Mayer•Group VP Marketing: Greg Worrell• Director, Customer Service Technical Support: Karine Apollon-Mowatt•Associate Director of Customer Service: Pat Drayton

To order more issues or for customer service: 1- 800-SCHOLASTIC

Library of Congress Cataloging-in-Publications Data available ISBN 0-439-39931-9

28 27 20 Printed in the USA. First printing X

My 100 Words to Read

Group 1

answer
believe
could
enough
knew
know
should
tell
these
those
told
would
write
wrote

Group 2

bought
bring
brought
buy
draw
drew
held
hold
hurt
laugh
talk
think
thought
walk

Group 3

above
around
because
behind
below
does
done
far
flew
fly
going
grew
grow
through
very

Group 4

always
it's
its
just
left
light
may
month
must
never
once
right
start
wrong
year

Group 5

away
call
find
found
full
kind
much
only
pull
put
round
shall
too
upon

Group 6

about
again
carry
city
clean
live
middle
own
ready
sure
though
warm
which
word

Group 7

beautiful
been
different
either
frighten
learn
neither
several
straight
today
together
tomorrow
trouble
yesterday

Which Word?

Directions:
Read the story.
Then answer each question with a blue word from the story. We did the first one for you.

1 "You won't believe what I'm going to tell you about William."

2 "I told you I don't like to hear gossip."

3 "Well, if I wrote it down then you could read it instead of hearing it."

4 "Even if you write it, it's still gossip."

5 "I knew that. Maybe I should just keep it to myself."

1. Which blue word is a homophone (a word that sounds the same, but has a different meaning) of the word **new**? knew
2. Which blue word is a homophone of the word **right**? ____________
3. Which blue word is the present tense of the verb **told**? ____________
4. Which blue word is the past tense of the verb **write**? ____________
5. Which blue word comes between **apple** and **car** in the dictionary?

   ____
6. Which two blue words rhyme? ____________ ____________

Jack's Shoes

Directions: Use the words in the **Word Box** to complete the story. Then follow the directions to solve the riddle below.

Jack __ __ __ __ __ (1) like new sneakers. __ (2) __ __ __ __ are his old sneakers. __ __ (3) __ __ (4) __ are the ones he wants.

Every time Jack goes up the hill with Jill, he falls down and breaks his crown. He __ __ __ __ (5) __ __ __ __ the problem is his shoes. Jack told me if he had a good pair, he __ __ __ __ (6) __ get to the top without falling.

Are new shoes __ (7) __ __ __ __ __ to help Jack? I don't __ (8) __ __ __ the __ (9) __ __ __ (10) __ __. But it could be that Jack is just clumsy!

Word Box

know	would	These	believes
Those	enough	answer	could

Now try this! To solve the riddle, look for the numbers below some of your answers in the story. Then fill in the matching letters below.

What wears shoes but has no feet?

__ __ __   __ __ __ __ __ __ __ __ __!

2 3 7   4 5 1 7 10 9 6 8

Dogs Can't Spell!

Directions:
Molly the Mutt has something to tell your teacher, but she can't spell very well. Can you help? Find and circle **eight** misspelled words in the letter. Then write them correctly on the lines. We did the first one for you.

1. should
2. ____________
3. ____________
4. ____________
5. ____________
6. ____________
7. ____________
8. ____________

From the desk of Molly the Mutt

Dear Teacher,

The first thing I shood say is that I'm sorry. Sort of.

Let me explain. I no there are times when a student comes to class without his or her homework. You ask where it is, and the student ansers, "The dog ate it!"

"Who wuold beleive such a story?" you say. "Please tell the truth."

Well, I'm righting this letter to tel you it's all true. I, Molly the Mutt, eat homework. Lots of it. I go from house to house, from state to state, gobbling homework.

It all started when I was just a puppy. That's when I tasted my first book report on *Green Eggs and Ham*. Delicious! Now, I'll eat anything I can get my paws on. I like stories, spelling tests, even math workbooks. I can't get enuff!

So the next time a student shows up with a scrap of paper covered in slobber, think of me.

Yours truly,
Molly the Mutt

Find the Word

Directions:
Complete the sentences below with words from the **Word Box**. Then find the words in the puzzle. Words may go across, down, or diagonally. We did the first one for you.

1. Have you <u>thought</u> about what you'd like for your birthday?
2. Hannah likes to ____________ home from school.
3. Last Friday, I ____________ a new notebook.
4. Today I will ____________ the notebook to school with me.
5. Ruthie and Carlos like to ____________ pictures of aliens.
6. May I ____________ your hand if I get scared during the movie?
7. Sometimes we ____________ too loudly in the library.
8. Tanya used colored pencils when she ____________that picture.

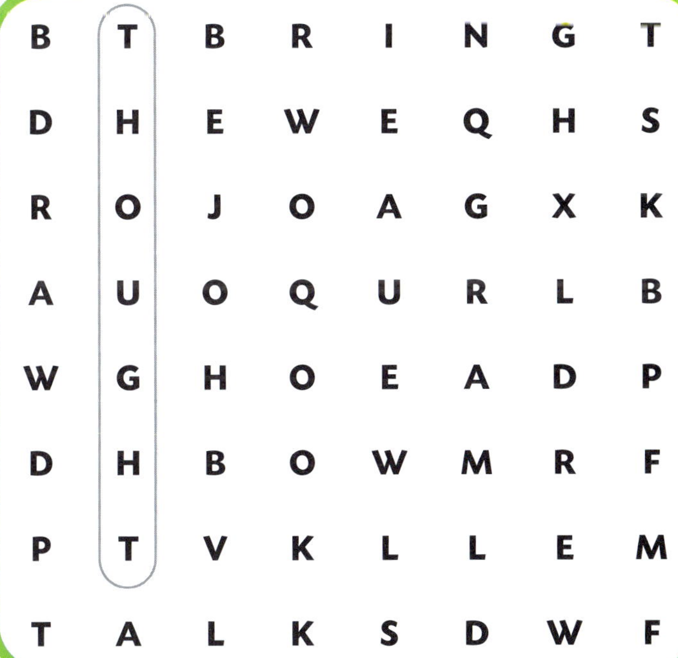

B	T	B	R	I	N	G	T
D	H	E	W	E	Q	H	S
R	O	J	O	A	G	X	K
A	U	O	Q	U	R	L	B
W	G	H	O	E	A	D	P
D	H	B	O	W	M	R	F
P	T	V	K	L	L	E	M
T	A	L	K	S	D	W	F

Word Box

bought	drew
bring	draw
~~thought~~	walk
hold	talk

Match It!

Directions:
A synonym is a word that has the same meaning as another word. Read the story. Then find the synonym for each blue word in the **Word Box.** We did the first one for you.

Word Box

think laugh talk ~~brought~~ held buy hurt

Justin took his pet pig, Hoggy, to school. He cradled Hoggy in his lap during class. Every time Ms. Lawrence started to speak, Hoggy started to oink! Ms. Lawrence didn't suppose it was such a good idea to have a pig at school. So Denise asked if she could purchase a rooster for the classroom instead. We all started to giggle. Ms. Lawrence laughed so hard her stomach ached!

1. took brought
2. cradled ________
3. speak ________
4. suppose ________
5. purchase ________
6. giggle ________
7. ached ________

A-maze-ing Verbs

Directions:
To complete the maze, pass only through the **correct** sentences. An incorrect sentence is like a wall in the maze: You cannot pass through it. The correct path takes you through **nine** boxes.

Pedal Puzzle

Directions: Use the words in the **Word Box** to complete the sentences below. Then write the words in the correct spaces in the puzzle. We did the first one for you.

Word Box

~~above~~	behind	because
below	far	very
around	through	

Across

3 When I ride my bike, the street is under my tires and the sky is above my head.

5 I have to put air in my tires __________ they are flat.

6 When you pump up your tires, make sure the air is coming __________ the hose.

7 We like to ride our bikes __________ in bigger and bigger circles.

Down

1 The distance from my house to my friend's isn't __________.

2 As I pedal, I can see the ground move __________ my feet.

4 Our neighborhood is a __________ interesting place to explore.

5 I ride in front and my friend rides __________ me.

A maze-ing Birds

Directions:
To complete the maze, pass only through the **correct** sentences. An incorrect sentence is like a wall in the maze. The right path goes through **seven** boxes.

Herman the Class Dragon

Directions: Use the words from the **Word Box** to complete the story below.

Word Box

around	flew
behind	grew
because	going
done	through
does	above

Our teacher returned from vacation with a very small dragon. We named him Herman ______________ (1) when we said "Herman" he flared his nostrils and looked like he was ______________ (2) to smile. We kept him in a big tank. That way, we could look ______________ (3) the glass and watch him sleep or reach his head ______________ (4) his body to lick his wings clean.

As Herman got bigger, his wings also ______________ (5). One of our class jobs was lifting Herman high ______________ (6) our heads so that he could practice flapping his wings. We would have one kid supporting his front and another ______________ (7) him. Afterward, we would pet Herman's scales and tell him he had ______________ (8) a good job. Practicing seemed to tire him out.

That is until last Monday, when Herman ______________ (9) up and perched on top of the highest bookshelf. He gave us a toothy smile the way he sometimes ______________ (10) and flapped his wings proudly.

Which Word?

Directions:
Read the story. Then answer each question with a blue word from the story. We did the first one for you.

Alisha always gets new sneakers at the start of the school year.

Today, Alisha picks up a sneaker that is blue with green stripes on its side. It's perfect. She asks, "May I try this on?"

A man checks the size of her right foot and then her left. Then he brings her the shoes. But when she puts them on, her feet hurt. "These don't fit," she says. That's when she sees that they are on the wrong feet!

1. Which blue word is a contraction of **it is**? it's
2. Which blue word means the same as **beginning**? ______________
3. Which blue word means the opposite of **never**? ______________
4. Which blue word is a homophone for **it's** and means "belonging to it"? ______________
5. Which blue word has the same spelling as a month of the year and means "to allow"? ______________
6. Which blue word has one syllable and means "12 months"? ______________
7. Which blue word means the opposite of both **left** and **wrong**? ______________

My Blue Monster

Directions:
Use the words in the **Word Box** to complete the story. Then solve the riddle at the bottom of the page. We did the first one for you.

Word Box

always	light	must	~~once~~
just	month	never	

I have a blue monster in my closet. About o n c(1) e a __ __ __ __ __(2) I move all the coats and shoes and go in for a visit.

He's __ __ __ __ __ __ a little cranky at first. "It's bad enough," he growls, "that you almost __ __(3) __ __ __(4) come to see me, but when you do, __(5) __ __ __ you let in all that __ __(6) __ __ __?" But then we play cards or a game of Clue and he cheers right up.

Then I say goodbye for another month or so. He __ __(7) __ __ growls and says, "Make sure you leave it good and dark when you go." But I know he'll miss me.

Now try this! Look for the numbers beneath some of the letters in your answers above. Then fill in the matching letters to solve the riddle below.

What do you do with a blue monster?

__ __ __ __ __   __ __ __   __p!
1 2 3 3 4   2 6 5   7

Mystery Letter

Directions:
In each set of words, the same letter is missing. Can find the mystery letter in each set? The letters you need are in the **Letter Box.**

Letter Box

t
e
h
r
b
a

1 ____ elow
____ ecause
____ ehind
The mystery letter is ____

2 yea ____
sta ____t
w ____ong
The mystery letter is ____

3 onc ____
n ____ ver
l ____ft
The mystery letter is ____

4 ____ lways
m ____ y
w ____ lk
The mystery letter is ____

5 i ____ s
jus ____
mus ____
The mystery letter is ____

6 lig ____ t
rig ____ t
mont ____
The mystery letter is ____

Now try this!

To answer the riddle below, fill in the six mystery letters in the order they appear above.

What can you hold without using your hands?

Your ___ ___ ___ ___ ___ ___!
1 2 3 4 5 6

Find the Word

Directions: Complete the sentences below with words from the **Word Box**. Then find each word in the puzzle. Words may go across, down, or diagonally. We did the first one for you.

1. I chose a pumpkin that had no bumps and was perfectly round.
2. Sarah had a question about her homework, so she picked up the phone to ____________ Tanisha.
3. After Juan ate the hot fudge sundae, his stomach felt very ____________.
4. When my mom went ____________ on a trip, she sent me postcards.
5. Miko's cat likes to sit ____________ her lap while Miko reads.
6. Sam had to ____________ on his dog's leash to keep him away from the hornet's nest.

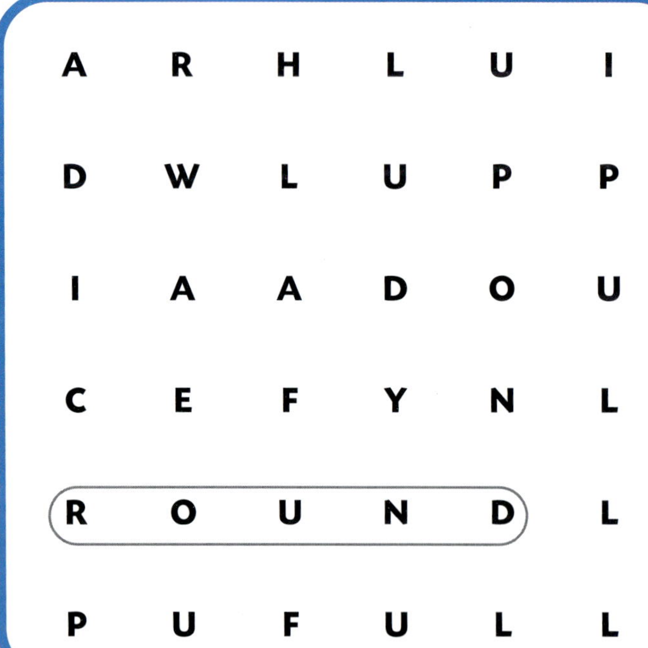

A	R	H	L	U	I
D	W	L	U	P	P
I	A	A	D	O	U
C	E	F	Y	N	L
R	O	U	N	D	L
P	U	F	U	L	L

Word Box

away	~~round~~
pull	full
call	upon

Lost and Found

Directions:
Read the story.
Then fill in the bubble next to the best answer to each question below.

One day Alisha's little brother found three dollars. "Look!" he said. "Now I can buy a pony!"

"I think a pony will cost too much," Alisha said. "Shall I help you find something to spend it on?"

"Okay," he said. He put the money in his pocket.

"Ice cream might be a good thing to spend it on," said Alisha. "What kind do you want?"

"I only like one kind. Chocolate," said her brother.

"I think chocolate is the best kind, too," said Alisha.

1. When Alisha says a pony will cost too much, she means:
   - ◯ a. Three dollars is more than enough money to buy a pony.
   - ◯ b. A pony costs a lot more than three dollars.
   - ◯ c. If her brother had found five dollars, he could buy a pony.

2. When Alisha says,"I think chocolate is the best kind, too," the word **too** means
   - ◯ a. also.
   - ◯ b. two.
   - ◯ c. not at all.

3. The opposite of found is
   - ◯ a. kept.
   - ◯ b. forgot.
   - ◯ c. lost.

4. Which word means the same as kind in this story?
   - ◯ a. nice
   - ◯ b. child
   - ◯ c. type

5. In the dictionary, the word only appears
   - ◯ a. between **lonely** and **quiet**.
   - ◯ b. after the word **totally**.
   - ◯ c. before the word **night**.

Sort It Out!

Directions:
Put each word from the **Word Box** in the circle where it belongs. We did the first one for you.

Word Box

~~found~~	find	behind
away	upon	pull
call	put	above
below	around	

Action Words

found

Direction Words

Now try this!

Write a sentence using as many words from the **Word Box** as you can.

How many words from the **Word Box** did you use?

Puzzle It Out!

Directions: Use the words in the **Word Box** to complete the sentences below. Then write the words in the correct spaces in the puzzle.

Across

1. My name was the first ___________ that I learned to spell.
3. Sam washed the dishes so they were sparkling ___________.
4. The weather today is ___________ but not hot.
5. At the end of second grade, our teacher said we were ___________ for third.

Down

2. Will you share my popcorn, or do you want your___________?
3. She has to ___________ the baby because he's too little to walk.
6. We had burgers for dinner last night, and we're having them ___________ tonight.

Word Box

carry	warm
own	clean
again	word
ready	

Loony Lunch Time

Directions:
Don't read this story yet! First, find a partner. One of you will read aloud the words under the lines at left and write down what the other says. Then put those words in the story and read it out loud.

1. ____________________ famous person
2. ____________________ adjective
3. ____________________ verb ending in *–ing*
4. ____________________ adjective
5. ____________________ noun
6. ____________________ noun (plural)
7. ____________________ animal
8. ____________________ two-digit number
9. ____________________ adjective

PAULETTE BOGAN VIA SODA

Lunch time at __________ (1) Elementary sure can get __________ (2). When the bell rings in the middle of the day, kids start __________ (3) toward the cafeteria. But I have to say, the food is usually __________ (4). I'm not sure which dish they serve most often. It's probably fried __________ (5) or macaroni and __________ (6). I should warn you, though. There is a rumor going around about the __________ (7) soup. People say it was made in 19 __________ (8). How __________ (9)! Next time you're in the city where I live, come on by and I'll treat you to lunch!

Bugs's Big Day

Directions:
A synonym is a word that has the same meaning as another word. Read the story. Then find the synonym for each blue word in the **Word Box**. We did the first one for you.

Word Box

about carried clean ~~lives~~ middle owns ready sure

My pet rabbit, Bugs, dwells in a cage in my backyard. I keep his cage spotless. I feed him and pet him. When my teacher said anyone who possesses a pet could bring it in for Class Pet Day, I was prepared! I toted Bugs's cage all the way to school on a city bus. It took around an hour but it was worth it. I put Bugs in the center of the room and everyone took turns petting him. I'm certain that Bugs was the world's happiest rabbit that day.

1. dwells lives
2. spotless ____________
3. possesses ____________
4. prepared ____________
5. toted ____________
6. around ____________
7. center ____________
8. certain ____________

A Winning Story

Directions: Use the words in the **Word Box** to complete the story below. We did the first one for you.

Word Box

either	Neither	~~together~~
several	been	yesterday
Today	tomorrow	different

Carlos and Anna play checkers together (1) almost every day. They play again and again. ________ (2) one likes to lose. Carlos has ________ (3) the winner ________ (4) times. When they played ________ (5), Anna won every game. ________ (6), ________ (7) one could win. Maybe they should play a ________ (8) game ________ (9)!

Now try this! Put the words in the **Word Box** in ABC order. We did the first one for you.

1. been
2. ________
3. ________
4. ________
5. ________
6. ________
7. ________
8. ________
9. ________

A Monstrous Maze

Directions: Read this ad for Fright Boosters Night School. Then complete the maze by passing only through the **true** sentences. The correct path takes you through **seven** boxes.

Attention, Monsters! Do you have trouble scaring humans? Has a little old lady ever told you you're beautiful? Do you sometimes worry that you couldn't frighten a small child?

Don't worry. Being scary isn't something you're born with. It's a skill you can learn. And at Fright Boosters Night School, we can teach you. Soon little old ladies will faint at the sight of you. Grown men will leap straight into the air at your growl—or your money back. Call today!

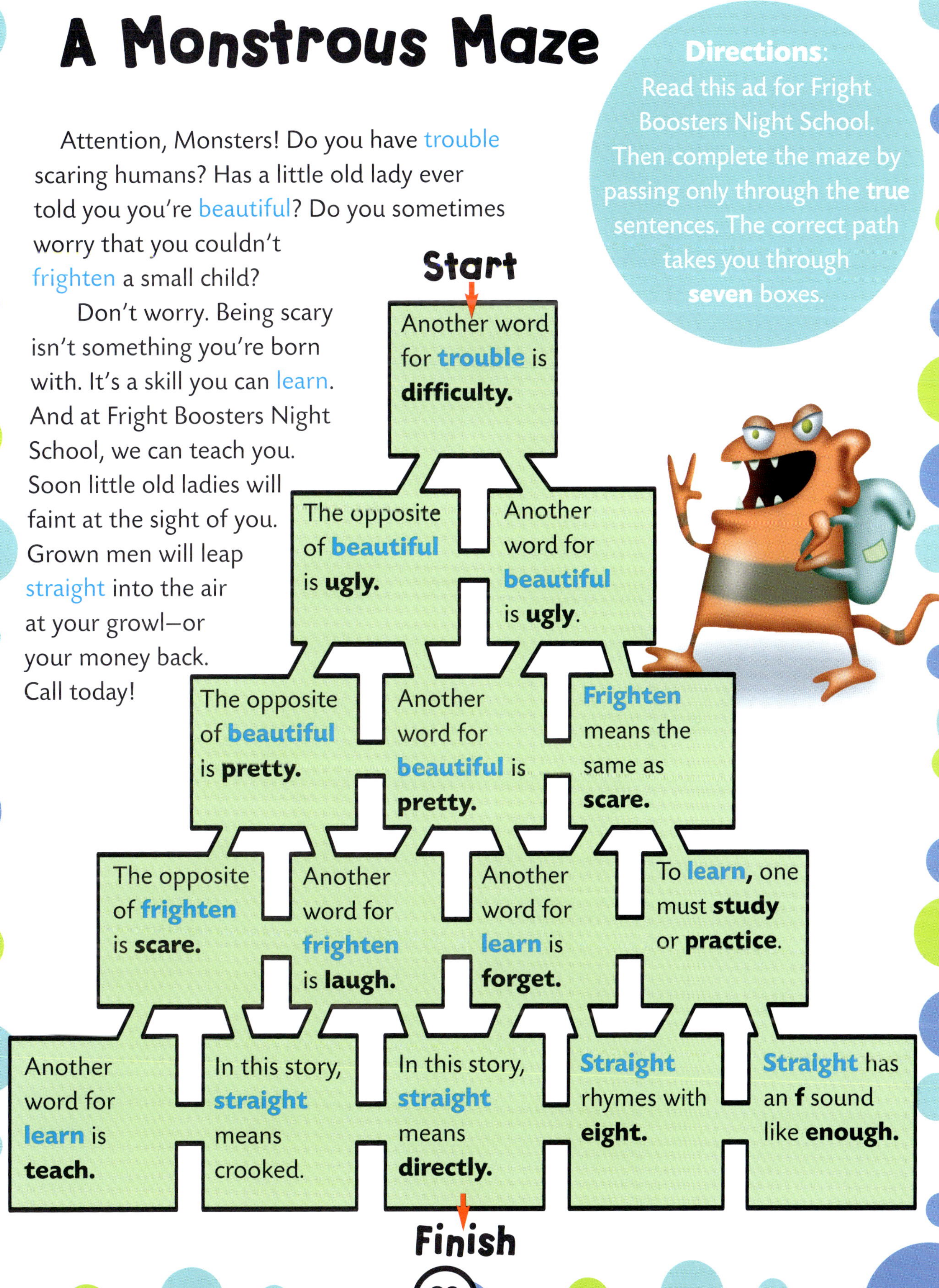

Aliens Can't Spell!

Directions: The alien who wrote this ad can't spell very well! Can you help? Find and circle **nine** misspelled words. Then write the words correctly on the lines below.

If you're from the planet Gooeygoopiter, listen up!

Do you have trubble with slime? Has it bin oozing from your ears and toes? When you get togehter with human friends, do your feet leave embarrassing gooey marks on their carpets?

What you are about to lern will change all of that. SLIME AWAY is the first slime remover made for stubborn problems like yours. Simply apply it to your toes and ears. Wait sevral minutes. Then watch as SLIME AWAY works its magic! You'll look and feel difrent right away.

Behind all that slime there's a beautifull alien! So why wait until tomorow when you can be slime-less twoday?

1. ______________ 4. ______________ 7. ______________

2. ______________ 5. ______________ 8. ______________

3. ______________ 6. ______________ 9. ______________

again	answer	beautiful
because	been	behind
brought	city	does
live	neither	once

Word Cards for Name That Word! game. See page 29.

Name That Word!

Name That Word!

Name That Word!

Name That Word!

Name That Word!

Name That Word!

Name That Word!

Name That Word!

Name That Word!

Name That Word!

Name That Word!

Name That Word!

pull	**several**	**shall**
start	**straight**	**tell**
thought	**through**	**tomorrow**
trouble	**warm**	**word**

Word Cards for Name That Word! game. See page 29.

Name That Word!

Name That Word!

Name That Word!

Name That Word!

Name That Word!

Name That Word!

Name That Word!

Name That Word!

Name That Word!

Name That Word!

Name That Word!

Name That Word!

Name That Word! Board Game

What you need to play:

- The game board on pages 30–31 of this book
- Word Cards (cut from pages 25–28 of this book)
- Two players
- A game piece for each player (like a coin or a button)
- One die

How to play:

- Place all the Word Cards facedown in a pile.
- Roll the die. Move your piece the number of dots on the die.
- If you land on a pink circle, say a word that rhymes with the word in the circle.
- If you land on "Pick a Card," your partner picks a Word Card and reads the word on the card out loud. You have to spell it. If you spell the word correctly, move ahead one space. After you follow the directions on that space, it is your partner's turn.
- If you land on any other circle, follow the directions.
- The first person to reach *Finish* wins!

More games you can play with the Word Cards:

Spelling Pile-up

- Put all the cards facedown in a pile.
- One player picks a card and reads it out loud. The other player has to spell the word.
- If that player spells it correctly, he or she gets the card. If he or she spells it incorrectly, the other player keeps the card.
- The player with the most cards at the end wins.
- You can also play this game with rhyming instead of spelling.

Memory

- Combine 12 of your cards with the same 12 of a friend's cards. (Use either all of your light blue cards or all of your dark blue cards.) Mix them up.
- Spread all of the cards facedown. The cards should not overlap.
- Pick a card and turn it over. Now pick another card and turn it over. If the two words match, take both cards and keep them. Go again until you turn over two cards that do not match.
- The other player does the same.
- The game is over when there are no cards left. The player with the most cards wins!

Name That

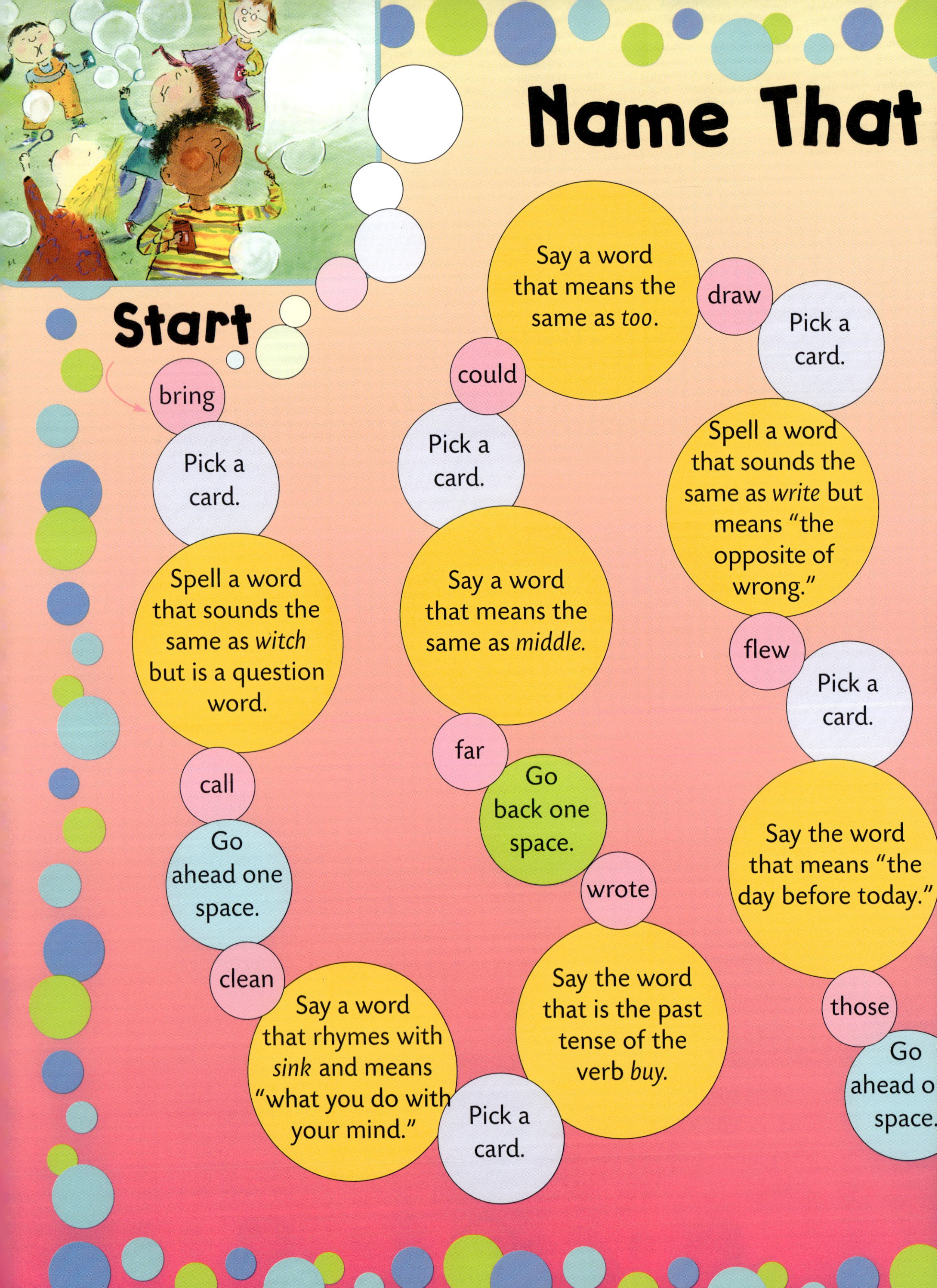
Start
bring
Pick a card.
Spell a word that sounds the same as *witch* but is a question word.
call
Go ahead one space.
clean
Say a word that rhymes with *sink* and means "what you do with your mind."
Pick a card.
Say the word that is the past tense of the verb *buy*.
wrote
Go back one space.
far
Say a word that means the same as *middle*.
Pick a card.
could
Say a word that means the same as *too*.
draw
Pick a card.
Spell a word that sounds the same as *write* but means "the opposite of wrong."
flew
Pick a card.
Say the word that means "the day before today."
those
Go ahead o
space.

lord!

Board Game (See page 29 for how to play.)

Say a word that means the same as *frighten*.

kind

may

Say a word that means the opposite of *laugh*.

Go back one space.

fly

Say a word that means the same as *done*.

Pick a card.

hold

Say a word that rhymes with *show* and means "to get bigger."

Spell a word that sounds the same as *no* but means "to understand."

Pick a card.

end

Say a word that means the opposite of *full*.

Say a word that means the opposite of *above*.

knew

Say a word that means the same as *below*.

Pick a card.

Say the word that is the past tense of the verb *hurt*.

Pick a card.

Pick a card.

much

talk

Say a word that means the same as "12 months."

light

Say a word that means the opposite of *found*.

Finish!

otes